My Walk!

By Arcadia Kuahuia

DORRANCE PUBLISHING CO
EST. 1920
PITTSBURGH, PENNSYLVANIA 15238

Dorrance Publishing Co
585 Alpha Drive
Pittsburgh, PA 15238
Visit our website at www.dorrancebookstore.com

ISBN: 979-8-88683-441-3
eISBN: 979-8-88683-421-5

My Walk!

By Arcadia Kuahuia

Okay, here we go!

Let me start by saying what I have been going through. In 2017 I was asked by a coworker (let's call him "P) "Do you believe in God?"

I said, "Yes!"

He then asked, "So you believe in the devil too?"

I said, "Yes!" And at times I eat lunch with the devil? The person asking the question was not asking the question to know whether I believed or not, but to make fun of me. My life has never been the same since!

During a training in Oahu, April 2017, a female coworker who sits next to P (let's call her Fatsetta) came up to me. Along with P, asked me, "Would you hit us if you found out we were making fun of you?"

I told them, "I would walk away before that happens, but if you pursue me, then it is all on you!"

May 2017—I saw another coworker watching a video of my husband's grandma's birthday celebration on YouTube. I had enough! I asked the supervisor about whether there was an investigation on me. He said no! I told him of what I saw. What my supervisor did not know was that I could hear his discussion with the assistant supervisor and the secretary, who was the one viewing the video. The supervisor told her, "I told you not to look at it." She was mad at me, and at that moment I knew it was not only two people making fun of me in my office, but there were also more. So, the harassment started. I filed a complaint with my supervisor in June 2017. The complaint was sent to Oahu, and an investigation was made, but the person who investigated retired within two weeks of the initial interview.

The harassment continued until I could no longer take it and called Fatsetta and P out on their actions. Police were called, and I told the officer of my former complaint, and he told me to file an injunction. I filed, but the judge said there was not enough evidence. Fatsetta and P filed a complaint against me. I got a letter two weeks later stating that an investigation was to be held regarding their allegations, threatening a coworker. I told the two people investigating the situation of what I did and what I called them. The new supervisor from Oahu informed me that they could not find any paperwork on my harassment complaint that was turned in in June. The person retired, and they could not find the notes I gave her. How convenient! The new supervisor from Oahu had no information of the paperwork; I gave the former supervisor regarding my original allegations. So, I made a copy for her and gave her my information. Even though I followed procedures and made the first complaint, I was now being accused of threatening a coworker. Everyone in the office knew the situation. I gave her a copy of the paperwork, to prove my original complaint and e-mail between me and the retired supervisor.

January 2018—I turned in my resignation, before I really snapped, and someone would have gotten hurt. I was already being investigated for threatening a coworker. As stated in my resignation, eight people were involved in the harassment. I had to leave my position because no one was listening to me, daily harassment continued, and they were now messing with my cases. I informed my superior of the daily harassment. The only thing that kept me sane was trusting in GOD. Every day I would pray before I go to work, for the LORD to help me to forgive the things they were doing to me. I would pray before work, during lunch, and again at night. At one point they sent in a person that spiritually hurt me. At that time, I did not know about spiritual battle. I heard of spiritual battle but never literally and physically been in one. This man walked in front of me, saying something under his breath, looking mad. he looked at me, spat on the ground, walked up the stairs, and walked past me. I was standing by the stairs. I felt something hit me on the left side of my face; my left leg buckled.

I had to hold on to the railing to keep my balance. I looked, but there was no one there. When I walked back into the office, I overheard "P" say, "Well, at least now we know."

Funny because that same day I saw people from my church waiting in the waiting room. I told them hi because they were my mom's friends. I also noticed a Kahu sitting in the waiting room, holding his puppy. They were trying to figure out which church I belonged to. I was so angry, but I could not do anything because of the allegations they had against me. Before I turned in my resignation, there was a week of daily incense burning in the office as well as the smell of alcohol coming from the air conditioner. Every day that I would come in, after lunch, or at times first thing in the morning. I would smell incense burning or alcohol in the air. They all knew I had allergies. And it was not only one person burning incense; they were taking turns. The smell came from different directions. My cubicle was in the center of the room. And funny thing is that the smoke did not set the smoke detector off, because we did not have any. LOL.

My sin was covering up for my husband who was wanted for a probation violation and protecting my son who had substance abuse problems and was being investigated of involvement in illegal activities. As of today, both situations have been addressed. And no one can no longer hold it against them. They are free!

John 8:36: *So if the son frees you, you will really be free!* (CJB)

2017—I had one of those bad days at work, where I heard discussions between my family and I being repeated at work. I was walking in Longs when I heard a voice ask, "Do you need help?"

I answered yes!

About a minute later, I heard a Longs worker ask if I needed help. I asked him a question about the product I was looking at. I did not pay attention to it then, but now I realize it was part of what I was about to experience. GOD answering my prayer. From that day on, I heard conversations at work that had to do with my family. They, P and Fatsetta, along with their minions could not understand how I could hear their conversations. They even thought I was using a miracle ear product in the office. Even at home I started hearing the chickens, and the dog barking, and I could understand what they were saying. There were instances where I would be listening to gospel music on my phone with my earphones on; the volume would get loud, by itself, in order to deafen me. They particularly did not like the songs "Spirit Move" and "The Same Power." I could hear Fatsetta say she is playing it again. Inside of me, I truly wanted to hear her squeal. 'Cause she would make a squealing sound whenever the music came on. Everything they did to me; I would talk to GOD about and continued to ask GOD to help me to forgive.

December 2017—I contacted the civil rights officer. She asked if it was a religious violation. At that time, I said no. I was looking at it as a regular office discrimination. I then tried to call the FBI. I left several messages; they never got back to me. Every time I called after that, my phone would disconnect. I know my family was being investigated, but no one wanted to tell me the reason why. They knew I would have to ask to see a warrant and who was making the allegations. What they did was a violation of my civil rights! I even recall a day when I was passing the *Tribune-Herald*, and I wanted to speak to a reporter. But I was fearful, so I went back to work. When I got to work, first thing, a meeting was held, and the supervisor informed everyone, "If you say anything to anyone, you will lose your job." I was flabbergasted. How did they know I was about to go to the newspaper? So, I just prayed.

Ephesians 6:12: *For we are not struggling against human beings, but against the rulers, authorities and cosmic powers governing this darkness, against the spiritual forces of evil in the heavenly realm.* (CJB)

December 31, 2017—Incident with my neighbor, announcing to the other neighbor what he was seeing in my house. I was devastated because I did not know they were seeing things that were going on in my house and in my bathroom. Then I got a text on my phone saying, "I'm sorry, I didn't know." The message just appeared on my cell phone with no contact number or name of who or where it came from. Yeah! Sounds as if I have truly lost my marbles; that's how I felt too.

It was not until January 31, 2018, that I sensed that I was going through things that were written in the Bible. I asked GOD to open my eyes, open my ears, and help me to understand. I started seeing flashes of light. I also saw the LION of Judah. Have you ever been praying, and you open your eyes, and you see the LION in front of you? And it is only for a moment. I even went walking at Liliuokalani Gardens, listening to gospel music. I finished my walk, got into my car, turned to my right to reverse, and whom do I see sitting in the back on the right back passenger seat? The LION of Judah.

One day, as I was napping, I opened my eyes and saw at the end of my couch, by my feet, a hooded figure, and its face was the face of an eagle. And I would see a man in the shower dressed in white, while I was bathing. I would see, in the dark, just eyes, which reminded me of the first time I saw a carabao (oxen). So, I went to the Bible, and, sure enough, found it in the book of Ezekiel and Revelation. The four living creatures. Also realized that the number I kept on seeing three and waking up at 3:33 a.m., had to do with the Bible. GOD = GOD the Father, GOD the Son, GOD the Holy Spirit.

Jeremiah 33:3: *'Call out to me and I will answer you- I will tell you great things, hidden things of which you are unaware.'* (CJB)

Ezekiel 33:3 *Now if , upon seeing the sword coming against that country, he blows the shofar and warns the people.* (CJB)

I belong to the Foursquare Church (Pentecostal). The book of Ezekiel is what our church is based on.

Pentecostal

Man—Jesus our Savior

Lion—Jesus, the mighty baptizer with the Holy Spirit and Fire

Ox—Jesus, the great burden bearer

Eagle—Jesus, the coming King

New Hope Symbols

Cross—Jesus the Savior

Dove—Jesus the Baptizer with the Holy Spirit

Cup—Jesus the Healer

Crown—Jesus the soon-coming King.

Dead Sea Scrolls

Man—Highest Intelligence, majesty

Lion—Spirit and Fire

Ox—Patience

Eagle—Speedy judgement

When I realized it was biblical, I was fearful, but as I read on and got to know ADONAI's promise, "Be strong, be bold, don't be afraid or frightened of them, for ADONAI your God is going with you. He will never fail you nor abandon you." (Deuteronomy 31:6 CJB), I started to get comfortable. Even my family thought I was losing it. Three times in 2018 I ended up in the emergency room. The first one was January 2018, for anxiety. They sent in a mental health specialist to speak to me; she went to UH with me, and she knew the atmosphere in the office. She confirmed that the atmosphere in my office was toxic; she had firsthand experience of dealing with the workers in the office. She would even come and complain to me about how they treated her clients, and I referred her to make a complaint to the supervisor. Second time I went in was March 2018. I went in because I felt like I could not breathe again. This time they placed me in the hallway, since they had no room. This time they just diagnosed me with UTI. I noticed that they were placing mental health patients in the hallway. I was disappointed because I was not going crazy, but who is going to believe that I am having an encounter with GOD? Went home, and two days later I felt my soul lift up out of my body and float over me. It went to the corner of the room. I asked my husband to take me to the hospital because I again felt as if I could not breathe. He told me, "Just relax and it will go away; you're having another anxiety attack." I did not listen. I called the ambulance. On the way to the hospital, my heart was racing. When I got there, they told me that my pressure was too high. So, they kept me in for observation. I fell asleep. When I got up, I saw a shadow filled with lights, looking at the computer at my medical chart. I was shocked. I looked around and I saw my daughter and my son's girlfriend asleep at the counter on the left side of my foot. I saw my son's girlfriend look up, and I thought she saw it too. She looked directly at it, as the nurse opened the curtain, but she did not make a comment. Then the nurse walked in. She looked at my medical records again and walked out.

Then I heard a voice say, "Let them help you."

I said, "If it is your will, LORD, it will happen. If not, it will not. In Jesus's name I pray. Amen." The nurse came back in and informed me that she was giving me medication and that I would be discharged in the morning.

I stayed with my son and his family for three days. On the second day, we were watching *Evan Almighty*. In that movie, he kept on getting up at a particular time. I realized, wait, as of June 2017, I was getting up every morning at 3:33 a.m. I asked my granddaughter to look up scriptures with 3:33. So I told her to look up scriptures with 3:33 and 33:3. Ezekiel 33:3 and Jeremiah 33:3 came up.

Ezekiel 33:3 *Now if, upon seeing the sword coming against the country, he blows the shofar and warns the people.* (CJB)

Jeremiah 33:3 *Call out to me and I will answer you- I will show you great things, hidden things of which you are unaware.* (CJB)

Ezekiel 36:26: *I will give you a new heart and put a new spirit inside you; I will take the stony heart out of your flesh and give you a heart of flesh.* (CJB)

Was my heart turning to stone, from the anger I was feeling towards my coworkers and disappointed that my family was thinking that I was crazy?

With all that I went through at work and my family not believing in me when I was telling them what I was hearing and seeing, I was very mad and disappointed. My family thought I was crazy. I even went to see a mental health specialist that my doctor recommended. And when I told her what happened at work and how I was feeling, you could tell that she was thinking I was crazy too. When I asked her if she believed in God, she said yes. When I asked her, What is your religion?" she said, "Methodist." When I asked her, "How often do you spend time with GOD?" she could not answer. At that moment I said to myself, "She is not going to be able to help you. She does not even know what is written in the Bible." I used to work in the mental health field, so I know what she was thinking. And especially an unbeliever. Never went back to see her again.

2 Corinthians 5:17: *Therefore, if anyone is united with the Messiah, he is a new creation- the old has passed; look, what has come is fresh and new!* (CJB)

Ephesians 4:24: *And clothe yourselves with the new nature created to be godly, which expresses itself in the righteousness and holiness that flow from the truth.* (CJB)

Colossians 1:22–23: *He has now reconciled in his Son's physical body through his death; in order to present you holy without defect or re-proach before himself-provided of course, that you continue in your trust-ing, grounded, steady, and don't let yourselves be moved away from the hope offered in the Good News you heard.* (CJB)

Ephesians 5:14: *Since anything revealed is light. This is why it says, "Get up sleeper! Arise from the dead, and the Messiah will shine on you!"* (CJB)

Titus 3:5: *He delivered us, it was not on the ground of any right-eous deeds we had done, but on the ground of his own mercy. He did it by means of the mikveh of rebirth and the renewal brought about by the Ruach HaKodesh.* (CJB)

Before going to the hospital in March 2018, I was asleep lying down on my loveseat, and I heard a voice say, "She gave birth." I heard them say, "He looks like you." I got up startled and upset. Again, how am I to explain spiritual birth? I never told anyone about this 'cause how am I to explain it?

John 3:5: *Yeshua answered, "Yes, indeed. I tell you that unless a person is born from water and the Spirit, he cannot enter the Kingdom of God."* (CJB)

I would see daily the flashes of light in my living room, and still see the LION of Judah, the Man dressed in white, and faces on the clouds. I even saw my parents' faces, like a movie on the clouds. One day, I was singing and praising the LORD, and I swear I saw my brother John sitting on the couch, just for a moment, in a blink of an eye. And when I looked in the mirror, my bathroom mirror, I saw my Mom, my sister Lita, and my sister Rose. All of them have passed away, even my Dad, all in a blink of an eye. My family were all baptized Catholic. My Mom, Dad, and I were baptized Pentecostal on February 14, 1988. John was a Jehovah's witness, Lolita remained Catholic, and I'm not sure if Rose remained Catholic.

1 Corinthians 15:52: *It will be but a moment, the blink of an eye, at the final shofar. For the shofar will sound, and the dead will be raised to live forever, and we too will be changed.* (CJB)

Matthew 16:27–28: *"For the Son of Man will come in his Father's glory, with his angels; and then he will repay everyone according to his conduct. Yes! I tell you that there are some here who will not experience death until they see the Son of Man coming in his Kingdom!"* (CJB)

Matthew 4:17: *From that time on, Yeshua began proclaiming, "Turn from your sins to God, for the Kingdom of Heaven is near!"* (CJB)

This is what I continued to write daily in my journal as an action and a prayer from November 2020 to March 2022.

Daniel 12:2: *Many of those sleeping in the dust of the earth will awaken, some to everlasting life and some to evertlasting shame and ab-horrence.* (CJB)

June 2018—I would pass graveyards and see shadows come towards me. One day, I was going to Minit Stop in HPP to buy something. As I was going up, I saw a hearse parked at the Mormon church. When I came down the road, I saw a figure dressed in white, with his face filled with lights, running out of the church. It passed the hearse that was parked on the side and came directly to my front passenger door. I was startled. All I could say was, "Blessed is he who comes in the name of the LORD!" (Baruch Haba B'shem ADONAI!)

Matthew 23:39: *For I tell you, from now on, you will not see me again until you say, "Blessed is he who comes in the name of ADONAI!"* (CJB)

Ephesians 4:24: *And to put on the new self, created to be like God in true righteousness and holiness.* (CJB)

May 2018—While at Kalae (South Point), about to take picture of the sunset. Saw a man in the clouds, looking at the people jumping off into the water. The man stood like my Dad. I took a picture of the sunset, could not take picture of the man on the clouds, for it lasted for only a moment. Continued every day, seeing faces in the clouds. Some I did not recognize; I just took it as being my ancestors. Evidence of my family watching over me.

June 2018—I saw a man sitting on my big Joe chair; he looked like my brother John. This happened while I was singing and dancing to the songs "Old Church Choir" and "Greater Is HE Who Lives in Me," again, in a blink of an eye.

Psalms 33:13—15: *ADONAI looks out from heaven; he sees every human being; from the place where he lives, he watches everyone living on earth, he who fashioned the hearts of them all and understands all they do.*

November 2018—Went to church weekly and sang in the church choir for about two weeks. One Sunday service, we sang a song with lyrics, "one day you'll open heaven for me." As I was sitting down during the service, I noticed the sky looked different; it was shaped the same way as the cloud I saw at Kalae. The clouds opened. Evidence of GOD opening the heaven for me. Also felt a breeze coming through the church, even when you can see the leaves on the trees were not moving. The shape of the clouds, an arch.

December 2018—At about three in the afternoon, I saw the biggest and brightest sun that I had ever seen. I went outside onto my porch to look at the sun, then I saw to the right of the sun a man dressed in full gold armor. He motioned with his left arm carrying the shield and said, "Come". From the left of the sun, a man dressed in white, riding a pale-white horse and carrying a white flag, rode across the sky. He passed the sun and the man. At this point I was afraid. I walked back into my house. And as I watched from my picture window, I saw a man dressed in white with a heart in the middle of his chest, like the picture my mom used to have of Jesus. I do not take medication, so I sure was not tripping! And I kept on telling myself, "I read this before," and sure enough, I found it in the book of Revelation.

Revelation 19:11: *Next I saw heaven opened and there before me was a white horse. Sitting on it was the one called Faithful and True, and it is in righteousness that he passes judgment and goes to battle.* (CJB)

Ezekiel 33:3–6: *Now if upon seeing the sword coming against the country, he blows the shofar and warns the people; then if the sword comes and takes away someone who heard the sound of the shofar but paid no attention to it, the responsibility for that person's death will be his own-he heard the shofar but paid no attention, so the responsibility for his death is his own; whereas if he paid attention, he would have saved his life. But if the watchman sees the sword and does not blow the shofar, so that the people are not warned; and then the sword comes and takes any one of them, that one is indeed taken away in his guilt, but I will hold the watchman responsible for his death.* (CJB)

Told NHEH, Women's Ministry of vision, in 2019 of Yeshua coming down from the sky. Posted comments on Twitter and Facebook on 2021, and informed two Bible groups. People are being informed.

January 2019—Started painting pictures that I photographed. My first painting was of Mauna Kea. Then painted my visions seven days later. In my paintings, clouds and landscapes would somehow have a face. One day, we went to Kona, took pictures of Hualalai Mountain. Before taking pictures, I noticed faces appearing on the clouds on the mountain. The waves were pounding that day and when ever I got close to the ocean, I would ask the waves to settle down. Also, I noticed that the rocks were shaped like a man lying down.

August 2019—I was feeling something go in me and come out of my forehead, had been feeling it since February 2019. I was also feeling something go to the bottom of my right foot. Was afraid to investigate it because it was something I have never heard about before except for the verse in the Bible about the eye of the needle.

So, I looked up the Pineal eye (third eye) and the verse in Luke 18:25—*It's easier for a camel to pass through a needle's eye than for a rich man to enter the kingdom of God!* (CJB) So I researched the third eye further. Found out that it is a Hindu and Buddhist belief. There are seven chakras—four upper body, governs mental properties, and three lower body, which is instinctual. Mine were going in me through the vagina and out Ajna (third eye). And funny thing is that the colors of the chakras are the colors of the rainbow. And rainbows are one of the things I like to take pictures of and are a covenant made by God with Noah, that he would never allow it to rain again, forty days and forty nights. All I know is what I feel; it is going in me and coming out through the third eye and sometimes through the Sahasvara (the crown, fontanel). And then I looked up the scripture about foot stool.

Luke 20:43: *ADONAI said to my Lord, "Sit at my right hand until I make your enemies your footstool."* (CJB)

And again, I was afraid. Is this really from GOD? I prayed about it, and I read the scripture.

2 Timothy 1:6–7: *For this reason, I am reminding you to fan the flame of God's gift, which you received through the s'mikhah from me. For God gave us a Spirit who produces not timidity, but power, love and self-discipline.* (CJB)

Again, my prayer—LORD, if this is of you it will happen, if not it will not. In Jesus's name, Amen.

John 3:5–6: *Yeshua answered, "Yes, indeed, I tell you that unless a person is born from water and the Spirit, he cannot enter the kingdom of God. What is born of the flesh is flesh, what is born of the Spirit is spirit.* (CJB)

September 2019—As I was passing the mirror, I saw a person that was mostly with white spots in me. The same as the one I saw in 2018 at the hospital, but this time, it was mostly white. Did I just see the HOLY SPIRIT in me? And I said to myself, "Are people seeing the HOLY GHOST?" Well, if they are, then they have no excuse. They definitely need to "Repent, for the Kingdom of GOD has come near."

November 2019—Went food shopping after dropping my son of at school. Saw a dark shadow shaped like a floating handkerchief come towards me as I passed a lady who was looking at a product. And it was not the first time I saw that happen.

When Roy's mom was in the hospital, we went to visit her. She was in pain, so I asked where her pain was. She said her stomach. I touched her stomach, and I saw a dark shadow like a snake wrap itself around my right hand and disappeared. Doctors X-rayed her stomach after that and said things were happening in her belly. She was battling pancreatic cancer; she was impacted, and after that, she was able to move her bowels.

This was the same time I saw my former classmate, and he, too, was battling cancer. As he smiled, I saw this sharklike teeth. Second incident: I saw a man I did not know; all I knew was that he had a badge that said, "Elder." A person from the Church of the Latter-day Saints. When I told him hi, he smiled, and I saw that same shark's teeth. And the same thing, the third time, on a friend of my son's girlfriend. As she was talking to him, his teeth were the same. I told her to please have your friend check on his health, because I saw something on him.

So, I went in search of the scripture that would explain what I am seeing.

Mark 16:17: *And these signs will accompany those who do trust: in my name they will drive out demons, speak with new tongues, not be injured if they handle snakes or drink poison, and heal the sick by laying hands on them.* (CJB)

Did I mention I was speaking in languages and seem to understand languages that I never spoke before? My second language is English. Tagalog is my native language, and I took Hawaiian language in college. But I would watch the news from Israel, and songs in Hebrew, and I would feel as if I understood what they were saying in Hebrew. I, at times repeated what they were saying in Hebrew eventhough I never spoke the language before.

January 2020—Woke up around 2:28 a.m. Mind you, every day I get up at around three a.m. and stay in bed until my alarm rings at four a.m.. Well, on this particular day, I looked at my phone and it said 2:28, so I went back to sleep. At three a.m., I felt something pierce my tongue, and a body settle in me. I thought to myself, "Is this what it means to be joined together or sealed?' It brought back memories of me getting married to my husband, a ring placed on my left fourth finger. But this one was different. I felt something piercing my tongue and a person settled in me. I asked GOD to help me understand.

Ephesians 1:13: *Furthermore, you who heard the message of the truth, the Good News offering you deliverance, and put your trust in the Messiah were sealed by him with the promised Ruach Hakodesh.* (CJB)

Ephesians 4:30: *Don't cause grief to God's Ruach Hakodesh, for he has stamped you as his property until the day of final redemption.* (CJB)

2 Corinthians 1:21–22: *Moreover, it is God who set both us and you in firm union with the Messiah; he has anointed us, put his seal on us, and given us his Spirit in our hearts as a guarantee for the future.* (CJB)

Revelation 7:3–4: *"Do not harm the land or the sea or the trees until we have sealed the servants of our God on their foreheads!" I heard how many were sealed-144,000 from the tribe of the people of Israel.* (CJB)

I have been sealed on my forehead.

Romans 8:1: *Therefore, there is no longer any condemnation awaiting those who are in union with the Messiah Yeshua.* (CJB)

Amen, Halleluyah!

March 2020—Went to visit my husband's aunty at the hospital. My husband, my son, and I prayed over her as she lay in bed, asleep. Nurse said she just gave her her medication and that she was tired. She opened her eyes for a little while when the nurse told her we were there, but she could not stay awake. As I was standing next to her bed, I could feel things. Then her nurse explained to us what was going on with her. I saw someone standing in the corner of the window. I felt and saw light and dark shadows as I touched her. At one point I had to tell my husband to lower his voice as he spoke to his cousin on the phone. I turned back to look at Aunty. I saw her spirit. She looked directly at me, and she said, "Help me."

I told her, "Aunty, it is okay. You can go when you are ready to go. For my GOD will take care of you." I also saw a shadow peeking through the privacy curtain, and I felt something go in my body.

She lasted for four months and passed away of liver and lung cancer. She had time to set things straight with her children. At one point I told her, "Aunty, do you believe in Jesus?" She said yes. I told her, "Then claim your healing." The next time we saw her, they said she was ready to go. The day I went to see her for the last time, her son was trying to get her ready for a bath. When she saw me, she wanted to stand up and come towards me. He instead told her to sit down at the edge of the bed, straightened her up so she could be more comfortable. When I hugged her, there was no sparkle in her eyes. I told her, "Aunty, it is okay, you can rest now. GOD will be with you." She died a day later.

2 Corinthians 5:8: *We are confident, then, and would much prefer to leave our home in the body and come to our home with the Lord.* (CJB)

April 2020—Easter Sunday. Went to my son's girlfriend's house to celebrate. My son was there, and everything was fine, until I heard breaking glass. My son and his girlfriend were having an argument. Saw a different person in my son. This was an old man with a small right eye (like he was squinting). That was not my son, and when I finally told him, "I rebuke you," his right eye opened.

My son stated, "You can't use Jesus on me; he doesn't work on me." Funny thing is, when my son mentioned Jesus's name, he finally calmed down and looked more like my son. I was not rebuking my child; I was rebuking the old man that was in him. Jesus took that abusive man out of my son. What I saw in him that night was his grandpa from his Dad's side of the family; he used to beat his wife. The old man that was in my son resembled his grandpa's boxing picture.

What I have been seeing:

Handkerchief-shaped shadow/snake = pain

Sharklike teeth = cancer

Dark shadow = fear/no relationship with Jesus

Old person = anger

Dressed in white = saved

Continued daily citing of shadows coming towards me. And I say, "Blessed is He who comes in the name of the LORD."

What I have been feeling:

Crown - saved

Forehead - reborn, renewal of the mind

Man out of the body - set free

Feet - foot stool

Daily vision of man dressed in white standing to the right of me, Lion of Judah to the right of me. What have I always prayed for, to be with GOD! Evidence of the Word of GOD being fulfilled in my life. Yeshua HaMashiach is ADONAI! (Jesus Christ is LORD.)

John 1:14: *The Word became a human being and lived with us, and we saw his Sh'khinah, the Sh'khinah of the Father's only Son, full of grace and truth.*

Romans 10:9: *That if you acknowledge publicly with your mouth that Yeshua is LORD and trust in your heart that God raised him from the dead, you will be delivered.* (CJB)

Matthew 10:32–33: *"Whoever acknowledges me in the presence of others I will also acknowledge in the presence of my Father in heaven. But whoever disowns me before others I will disown before my Father in heaven.* (CJB)

Philippians 2:10–11: *That in honor of the name given Yeshua, every knee will bow, in heaven, on earth, and under the earth- and every tongue will acknowledge that Yeshua the Mashiach is ADONAI—to the glory of God the Father.*

Christians (Blue Letter Bible)

Atmospheric Heaven—air that we breath as well as the space that immediately surrounds the earth (troposphere) twenty miles above the Earth.

Celestial Heaven—outerspace or stellar heaven. It includes the Sun, Moon, and stars.

Heaven of Heavens—heavenly spheres beyond which is not visible from the earth. Where God resides.

Summer 2019—My husband and I went to Maunakea. I was standing on the hill across the visitor center, and I was singing, "Go tell it on the mountain that Jesus Christ is LORD!" I was taking picture of the landscape, saw a man in front of me in the clouds with a Hawaiian helmet on, and a woman lying down on top of Maunakea with her face facing the top of the mountain where the telescopes are. I thought of nothing about it. Because before that, I saw a man at the bottom of the hill going up saddle road who was dressed like the signs of Kamehameha.

Most of the faces that I see in the clouds are at the same elevation as where I sang the song. Again, Yeshua Hamashiach is ADONAI! (Jesus Christ is LORD!)

I have seen people go from darkness into light.

Ephesians 5:8: *For you used to be darkness; but now, united with the Lord, you are light. Live like children of light.* (CJB)

Color of the souls

Dark - fear, no relationship with Jesus

Dark with lights - starting to know Jesus

Gray - lukewarm

White - believer, following Jesus

White with lights - redeemed

So far, I have seen three people who have turned into lights and went straight up to Heaven. One of them was my brother John. The other two are from my church.

June 2021 — I dreamt of leaving a child in the car. I went out of the car to speak to someone, and then I looked up at the sky. The sky was not blue; it was brownish/bronze, and so I hurried back to my car, but it (the sky) fell on me. And when it fell, it was ashes. I told my husband about my dream and my sister Jo. This is before the fires in California started happening. My sister lives in California. Mind you, this is the first time in a long time that I have dreamt.

Ending of the month, I walked into my friend's workplace in the mall. I was shocked to see that they sold satanic shirts, caps and witchcraft books. I asked her if people actually buy these, she said "yes". She said they have been selling it for ten years. I asked if she's into it. She said "no" Told her the only thing I liked was the cap that said "Not today Satan". When I said it out loud to her, I saw a shadow come off her and run to the back room. Amen and Halleluyah! Two weeks later, I went to check if she still had the products in there. The products were gone, and the store looked brighter, instead of being so dark.

James 2:19 You believe that "God is one"? Good for you! The demons believe it too- the thought makes them shudder with fear!

Mark1:27 They were all so astounded that they began asking each other, "What is this? A new teaching, one with authority behind it! He gives orders even to the unclean spirits, and they obey him!

Acts 2:17" "ADONAI says: "In the Last Days, I will pour out from my Spirit upon everyone. Your sons and daughters will prohesy, your young men will see visions, your old men will dream dreams.

March 2022—Dreamt of seeing a cement wall to the left side of me. In the back of me, my daughter, and my husband, was a wall of water, higher than the cement wall. Roy was to my right, and Rachel was to my left. I hung on to Rachel as the wall of water approached us from the back and went over us. I woke up startled.

I was reminded of this dream when I saw the news about the waves going over the building in Kona on July 18, 2022.

Revelation 22:16–17: "I, Yeshua, have sent my angel to give you testimony for the Messianic communities. I am the Root and Offspring of David, the bright Morning Star. The Spirit and The Bride say, "Come!" Let anyone who hears say "Come!" And let anyone who is thirsty come-

let anyone who wishes, take the water of life free of charge." (CJB)

2 Corinthians 6:16: *What agreement can there be between the temple of God and idols? For we are the temple of the living God- as God said, "I will house myself in them, …and I will walk among you. I will be their God, and they will be my people.* (CJB)

Romans 15:13: *May God, the source of hope, fill you completely with joy and shalom as you continue trusting, so that by the power of the Ruach Hakodesh you may overflow with hope.* (CJB)

My son Nathan asked me one day, "Why are you so happy?" My answer: "Because I have Yeshua in my life!"

I am fully trusting that GOD will accomplish what he promised and thankful that he is in my life.

YESHUA HAMASHIACH IS ADONAI!